The Tree

J.J. Smiley

Published by J.J. Smiley, 2022.

THE TREE

First edition. November 13, 2022.

Copyright © 2022 J.J. Smiley.

ISBN: 979-8215869963

Written by J.J. Smiley.

Table of Contents

The Tree

A collection of stories and rhymes having values of everyday life. To be read to, or by younger children. Each story or rhyme is a theme of caring, sharing, or introspection and finding appreciation of the things around us.

The Tree

It really doesn't take so long
To see a tree, grow big and strong
I watched my Dad once plant a tree
I think that I was only three
He said that tree was just for me.

It grew and grew and leaves it made
To let me play under its shade
The branches grew and got much longer
Every year the tree got stronger.

I love that tree; it is the best
The birds do too, to build their nest
In the fall, the leaves came down
We'd rake them up, but dad would frown
But then I'd play in red and yellow
When I was still a little fellow.

And after all the snow was gone
I'd see that tree upon the lawn
And watch for buds so small and green
A great big smile when they were seen

There's only one thing that can mean.

That summer's very, very near
That time of year we all hold dear
When air is warmed by the summer sun
And I can really have some fun
In the shade of that old tree
That was planted just for me.

Dragon Tears

Dryndle snapped furiously at the fly buzzing near his face. Again and again, he came ever so close to capturing it. He had been sleeping sweetly with great pleasure dreams floating in his head when the fly decided to walk about his nose and break his sweet dream at its high point. Several times his split tongue extruded out to swipe his muzzle. Each time the fly eluded the tongue. Finally, he had to retreat from the beautiful feeling of warmth and security that his parent had taught him to dream about when he was in his sleep state.

When he opened his eyes, he could see the insect buzzing in circles around the side of his face looking for a place to land. When it did, he snapped his infantile jaws at it, trying desperately to end the annoyance, get a small snack, and return to sleep. But the small fly evaded his every move, and Dryndle jumped up to gain the advantage, running as he snapped, catching only the air, only to trip and fall head over heal, adding insult to injury.

The limb he had tripped over was his parent's front claw, and now she too was out of sleep state. She looked down at the infant lying upside down and slightly tangled in its own tail and wings. Her enormous head nuzzled the infant and gently untangled the tail from on top of him. Then, with another nudge and a twist, she flipped him right side up. Dryndle looked around and gave a shake. The fly was nowhere to be seen.

He looked up at his parent and gave a sigh, and with a shake that went down his entire body ending with a snap of the end of his tail, he bounced off.
Dryndle played with the others his age, and the days and years went by quickly. He had now grown to adolescence and had developed into a handsome creature. As time went by, Dryndle's awareness of some of his friends changed. He grew fond of one friend, in particular; her name was Pica.

Pica was from a family fifteen valleys south of his own. She had skin of soft pink like that of the Healers. She would often be at the gatherings and being around her always seemed to fill him with a nervous tickle. At the gatherings, they would walk off together, and she would tell him the Human and Fairy stories she heard from her parent. Pica's parent was the Story Wise teller of her clan, as someday she, too, would be.
Pica wanted Dryndle to be with her, so she would tell the stories and, in so doing, would spellbind Dryndle for hours. She did not care if any others would join them; her thoughts were only for him.

Dryndle had heard many stories. One such story from the Story Wise was about the Shakesetter flower; this was his favorite. The flower grew in the Halsaid world, that place that was between his world and the Notails. The Notails were where the two-legged creatures lived, and the Halsaid was the thin area that kept the two worlds apart. The Shakesetter flower had the magical power to make another heart yours forever, but it could only be found deep in the Earthsplit where the shores of the Halsaid began. Unfortunately, many dragons died in the Earthsplit when fighting the notails. With the war over, dragons knew never to go near the Earthsplit.

Another young dragon named Graystrym had been coming around the gatherings and was showing off his wings. The clans said that finer wings than his had not been seen for ten millennia. Pica, too, was impressed with these wings. She and the other young dragons would stare intently as Graystrym would unfold his beautiful gossamer wings and send cool air currents toward the group. Dryndle thought otherwise; he insisted that Graystrym was only stirring up dust. It was clear that Dryndle was a little jealous, and Pica hoped it would move him to be more assertive toward her.

One day Graystrym was flapping and flirting with Pica, and she was very, very taken up with his advances, or so Dryndle thought. But unfortunately, he had average wings and was not so forward with his advances. So, he pondered what he could do to win her over when the thought occurred to him that he could give her a Shakesetter flower. That would be the way he could win her affection forever.

The following day he flew forty valleys to the west, and the land below became flat and sandy. He kept flying for what seemed a long time. The ground seemed hazy and not clear enough to discern, almost as if the earth was turning into clouds. The farther he flew, the closer the clouds rose up to him, and finally, they surrounded him. Finally, in a panic, he tried to descend to the ground. He dropped for the longest time, feeling gently for the earth by allowing his tail to precede him. Then, suddenly, the clouds went away, and he could see the ground below, but it was far down. Dryndle thought it must be another mile down before he could reach the ground.

The view below was not what he expected. The earth was green and lush, with many strange animals moving about and small feathered dragons with pointed mouths and short tails flying about. Shortly, he was on the ground. He was mystified. Could this be Halsaid, he wondered. He looked about and saw beautiful fields of golden grass edged by large trees with large green leaves. Pink and white flowers were growing by the trees, and he went to inspect them, hoping to find the Shakesetter.

When he got to the edge of the field, he saw that behind the trees and the flowers, there was a red glow. The glow came from the edge of a crevasse in the ground, and when he looked down into the hole, he saw a shoreline as if the crevasse was an opening like the entrance to a cave. He then realized that this was the edge of the Halsaid edge somewhere near, perhaps down in the hole, the Shakesetter would be his for the picking.

Carefully he climbed down in the crevasse. Looking around, he saw many plants and trees similar to the ones in his world. Then, looking among the flowers, he saw a fantastic sight. A stem appeared tipped with feathers; he saw another, and another they were appearing all around him. He was dazzled. Then with an astounding amount of pain, he saw one of the stems appear in his arm. Then, looking up, he saw a small tailless dragon running toward him with a larger stem, more like a branch, a bent branch with a stem laid across it then the stem disappeared. His eye caught the flight of the stem as it hurled through the air toward him, then he saw the gleaming point at the front of the flying stem, shaped like a tooth, and its sharpness gleamed in the light. He knew what a tooth was used for, and he put the tooth and the new pain in his arm together.

He ran and extended his wings as fast as he could. Some of the stems punctured the skin of his wings, tearing small holes but passing through the wing material. He banked left and came back around the little dragon from the rear. He took a deep breath and let out a tremendous roar, and much to his surprise, a fairly large fireball came from his mouth and landed quite close to the little dragon knocking it to the ground, unconscious. With the threat eliminated, he settled to the floor of the woods and cautiously walked over to the limp body of the little dragon.

He could not believe his eyes; it wasn't a little dragon at all. The creature had two legs but no scales and two arms again with no scales and absolutely no wings. The rest of its body was covered with scales, but the scales were not attached to the skin; part of the scales were separated from the skin. The skin was slightly brown and covered with darker hair. Some other covering was on its head as well as its feet. He sniffed the creature and was repulsed by the musky damp odor. The creature wasn't moving, and Dryndle no longer had any interest.

Dryndle did remember what he needed to find and wanted to be on his way home. Looking about the edges of the nearby field, he spotted a strange-looking flower and walked over to it. Its aroma was sweet and pleasant and warmed his inner heart. He was mesmerized by the scent and color. He picked several bunches and held them to his nose, inhaling deeply. This was indeed the flower for which he had come. Then, Dryndle's eyes widened, and his muscles tensed, along with the flowery fragrance mingled with the musky odor of the creatures.

He turned and jumped back just in time to avoid being hit by a creature's weapon. This weapon was not a stem but a long pointed shiny tooth the size of the creature's length. And then there were several creatures all around him swinging and stabbing at him. He was cut in the tail several times and then in the legs and soft underbody tissue. He was backing up frantically but was slowed by the trees. The creatures had pushed him away from the clearing and into the woods. He couldn't open his wings. He couldn't get a deep breath. He fell on his back, and the creatures kept swinging and stabbing, his blood was seeping out the wounds, and he thought he was going to die.

He wiggled and writhed; suddenly, he had backed into the smallest of clearings, just large enough to swing his tail around and in front of himself. Several creatures were knocked to the ground, opening up a free area leading back to the large field. Dryndle ran as fast as he could, disregarding the pain in his body. He entered the field, spread his wings, and lifted off the ground. He was thinking about throwing some fire again when several stems hit him in the neck, and the only thing he wanted now was to be home.

He traced his path from the air and found where he had entered this land. He flew down and climbed back the way he had come. He knew he was safe now, but he had lost much lifeblood and felt very tired. He still had one thing to do.

He landed back at Pica's hill, his life all but spent, holding the one Shakesetter flower he had managed to hold on to during the attack. He could barely push the flower toward her as she flew up to him. She was panic-stricken, and the grief of seeing him in such a terrible condition was overwhelming.

Tears started in her eyes, and she tried to lift him up to stand but couldn't. She looked down again and saw the flower. "Dryndle," she said, "My heart was always yours, and it needed no magic to secure it for you." As Pica's tears fell on Dryndle, he smiled through the pain and was slowly passing to the Afterrealm; now, his pain left both his body and his heart. He felt like he was slipping away, but when he opened his eyes again, Pica was there.

He realized at that moment that Pica was a healer, not a storyteller, just like her pink skin had foretold, and each golden tear that landed on him was repairing his broken body. So, he lay in her arms as more tears fell, and he wondered to himself what fine adventures they would share in the years to come?

The Birds

The Robin scoots along the ground
Listening, feeling for the sound
Of bugs and worms and other things
To quench the hunger that it brings.

A little Finch flits through the trees
Grabbing every bug, it sees
All morning long, they hop on by
Catching meals while on the fly.

Some birds look and sound like bees
Humming along but not in trees
They buzz along, and at each flower
Drinking nectar to gain more power.

All birds take turns to warm their nest
Many eggs are under the breast
So, after days, the eggs will hatch
And each tiny chick will be a match.

They'll peep and squeak and want their food
Mom and Dad must feed the brood

And all the birds must do the same
Gathering food is no game.

They must go out and find enough
To help their chicks grow big and tough
So they can grow to fly away
And have their own small chicks someday.

Shoes

I wish that I could tie my shoe
Not knowing how makes me blue
I've tried and tried with all my might
I just can't seem to do it right.

It's only a shoelace. It's just a string
I just can't make that loopy thing
You need to loop and go around
Another loop then makes it sound.

I tried and tried, and then one day
I looked down and shouted HEY!
It worked, It worked I did it right
Dad, come see it's quite a site.

The lesson here is just to try
If you fail, you won't die
Over time you will find
Success will come; you'll be just fine.

Bonnie and Clyde

Outlaws, criminals, vandals, they had been called many things, but good was not one of them. Their knack for getting in trouble was gaining notoriety. Not a day went by that didn't put them at odds with someone. If they kept it up, it was clearly understood their days would be numbered.

Bonnie went to the window and stared out carefully from behind the curtain. Her eyes would dart furtively at anything moving. She searched the yard and the neighborhood beyond. She watched for the longest time. Between each tree, behind each bush, at the corner of every house, someone could be coming. Yet, there were no suspicious movements, nothing to be seen; the neighbors had all left for work. Deserted, for now, no one walked the streets. What she thought no one could know. Her lips remained sealed in silence.

Clyde came up next to her and peered out as well. Then, seeing nothing to worry about, he left without saying a word. He was hungry; he went to look for something to eat.

Bonnie eventually left the window as well. She was bored. They hadn't had any excitement for days. She found Clyde stuffing himself and shoved him out of the way to get her share. Indignant at her bullying behavior, Clyde turned away and left the room.

Clyde had been up most of the night. He sat in the basement chair and yawned. Minutes later, in modest comfort, he fell asleep. An hour later, Bonnie came downstairs and eyed the sleeping Clyde. She was feeling both bored and playful. Bonnie crept to the chair and gave Clyde a sharp slap. Now startled and angry, Clyde felt retaliatory and immediately jumped out of the chair to respond to her challenge. Bonnie ran to the next room with Clyde in hot pursuit.

Clyde caught Bonnie quickly, and the two wrestled, knocking down everything in the room. Bonnie slipped out of Clyde's grasp and ran upstairs. Clyde again chased after her. Caught once again, Bonnie did everything she could to ward off Clyde's aggressive response. Tables toppled, and vases broke.

Later, the two sat out of breath, quietly recovering from the turmoil of the match. Neither had won, and both were exhausted. They looked at each other with pensive stares in silence.

Suddenly, fear gripped them; they both were attentive to the sounds. The rustling lock, the turning doorknob, someone was surely coming through the door. They ran cautiously to the back of the house, anticipating who was invading their hideout. They were ready to defend themselves but escape as well if need be.

Yes! They were flooded with relief. Fortunately, it was who they expected; no one else would have been tolerated. Joy came across their minds, for as silent as they had been all day, they couldn't help but burst out in sheer delight. Purrs and trickling meows filled the air. Both cats, circling the feet of the intruder as they rubbed against his legs, were ecstatic that their owner was finally home again.

"And what trouble have you gotten into today, may I ask?" he said to them.

Bonnie and Clyde are rescued cats, brother and sister. Initially, I gave them their names only as a joke. Well, it turns out they're very appropriately named. So, the joke's on me.

The Slugger

I swung the bat. I hit the ball
cause from the T, it could not fall
It went so high I cannot see
how far it went, where can it be.

Just start running, is what they said
My legs feel like the weight of lead
Look at the coach; he will know
where to send me, where to go.

He points to second and says go there
I'm sure I haven't got a prayer
He points again says go to third
Now I'm flying like a bird.

I can't believe my luck at last
I gave that ball a mighty blast
And not a moment did I think
that the other team would stink.

He says keep running; go on home
My mom is screaming on the phone

Dads taking pictures; he's the one
who told me this would be such fun.

But up till now, it's been a chore
never hitting, its' been a bore
I finally figured out this game
and if we lose, I'm not to blame.

I slide and watch the catcher's mitt
If I'm tagged out, I'll have a fit
But yes, I'm safe; we have a run
This kind of game is too much fun.

I'm sorry I complained so much
You said just try, don't use the crutch
about how shy I seem to feel
I'll find out that it's no big deal.

I'm glad you pushed and made me try
But I thought at first, I'd surely die
I learned the game; I took a chance
Now for you, I'll do, my victory dance.

The Apple Tree

This tree has limbs so near the ground
With apples growing big and round
I could climb it; it's not so tall
But if I did, I might just fall.

I tried and tried to shake the tree
But it's much too strong for me
The fruit won't fall, down to the ground
Those juicy apples, sweet, red, and round.

I know these apples are a prize
Their big and sweet, I must surmise
I'm too short to reach the fruit
A taller man, I must recruit.

I count ten apples from where I stand
I'll get my dad; he'll lend a hand
My dad is tall, at least ten feet
He could reach them. I'll have my treat.

He came and picked the fruit for me

He could reach all I could see
I washed them off before I ate
Made sure no bugs were on my plate.

I ate two; that's all I could
Boy, those apples were really good
The rest of them I gave to mom
She made a pie; it was da bomb.

We ate the pie right after dinner
I ate so much, not getting thinner
Tomorrow I will look for more
I know some people who're really poor.

They don't have an apple tree
In their yard, just like me
I can share with those who need
Mom said it is the greatest deed.

MAD

I'm really mad. I'm mad at dad
I'm so mad it makes me sad
To think that being mad is bad
Even though I'm just a lad.

Mom said I can't go in the pool
I thought this would be just so cool
I could swim and play the fool
But no, she said I can't be cool
So now I'm mad but not at dad.

The teacher said that I can't talk
She said that I can't take a walk
She said that I must use the chalk
Do the math and do not balk.

But now I'm stuck for all to see
The angers building up in me
I'm so mad but not at mom and not at dad.

Now I want to ride the bike

But I can see a lightning strike
I want to go outside and play
Just like I do any other day.

But the rain just keeps pouring down
Now my face is just a frown
I'm so mad but not at teacher, mom, or dad.
I didn't take some good advice
Cause I wasn't being very nice
They said I shouldn't climb the tree
They said I'd fall and break my knee.

Hospital beds are not so bad
But still, I lay here very mad
Not at nature, mom or dad
It's me this time that makes me mad.

What's the point of being mad?
Why should I always be so sad?
I'll change my ways and not be bad
Then I'll always be so glad
That I'm never ever mad.

The Chronicles of an Alien Child

The Federation mining ship was surveying a debris field in the Andarian cluster. It was believed to contain large amounts of Metalite. The debris field was made of remnants of a solar system destroyed when its star went nova half a millennia ago. The ship sensors found vast quantities of the ore it had been sent to gather.

The ship also located several metal boxes containing artifacts of a long-dead civilization. In those boxes were several books written in an altogether strange language. The boxes and their content were returned to the Federation Science Center for study. Among the many books that were studied, one, in particular, gave evidence to a hitherto unknown mystery, the origin and history of an alien child.

***

After climbing the tallest tree in Avdanoork, Bobi wrapped his feet around the highest limb and perched himself to watch the sunset. Three moons Ank, Fet, and Teta, had already risen above the horizon. The setting sun and the three rising moons in the pale yellow sky gave the landscape an eerie golden glow. The land was beautiful, but Bobi surveyed only the sky, watching as the stars began to shine in the early dimness. He sighed. He was never quite sure why the stars intrigued him, but he was confident that someday it would be revealed.

Bobi and his family lived on a mountainside east of the plains of Ank, named for the largest moon of Avdanoork. From the mountainside, the plains appeared grayish white; the color came from the Pic grass that grew everywhere. Here and there, Gryps could be seen grazing in small herds.

The mountainside was full of trees, many different species to be sure, and one stood out above all the rest, the Oaka. Sparse in number, they were, but very wide, wide enough to build and walk upon, with limbs extending many paces in every direction. The first limbs jutted out far above the tallest of animals on Avdanoork, thus affording the tree safety from being stripped of its leaves. If the Oaka survived the first hundred cycles without being destroyed, then its life was guaranteed to live for many hundreds of centuries. Bobi's family lived in a tree that was 5000 cycles old.

Bobi was only three cycles old and was allowed to explore his world. His world, as explained by his mother, consisted of any branch of their Oaka. Bobi thought it might take a lifetime to explore such a place. Instead, many days were spent exploring, and Bobi found new things to learn every day. The Oaka was so old and large that it was its own ecosystem. Insects and small animals evolved in the Oaka as if it were its own continent.

One day while on a high limb, Bobi looked down and saw his father carrying his brother Yabuut on his shoulder. Bobi's father sunk his claws deep into the bark and climbed quickly up the tree. Bobi scurried down from a higher limb to meet them. Bobi's father gently laid Yabuut in his bed. Yoda's mother began applying an ancient salve to Yabuut's wounds. Bobi entered the room quietly, listening to the conversations of his parents. Father had explained that Yabuut had not paid attention to where he was and strayed too close to a Wasa nest. As a result, the insects swarmed over Yabuut before he could do anything. Yabuut lay on the bed unconscious while Mother applied more salve to each swollen lump where he had been stung. Father said the ointment might help, but only time will tell.

Bobi's young mind felt only hate for the Wasa. His parents left the room, and Bobi ventured closer to his brother. Bobi moved his hand toward the swollen bumps on his brother's arm. His finger edged closer to a bump; he wanted it to go away. As his finger touched the lump, it slowly started to shrink. Bobi's eyes widened in surprise. He pulled his finger away and scrutinized it. It looked like any other finger. It looked just like his brothers or his fathers. He placed his finger near another bump. It, too, began to shrink. He continued to do this for a dozen more bumps with the same success.

Bobi was starting to feel weak, and he could hear his parents approaching. While he was happy that he could help, he was still apprehensive about this newfound skill. He left and went to his own room.

Bobi pondered how to repay the Wasa; later in the afternoon, he did something he had never done before. He climbed down the Oaka tree. On the ground, he found the feeling of soil and grass beneath his feet quite strange. It was as if he was sinking with each step he took. The hardness of the Oaka was all he had ever known.

Bobi hadn't wandered far before he heard a distant buzzing. He followed the sound and came to a crusty-looking bag hanging low to the ground beneath a tree. He could see the insects coming and going from a small hole in the bottom of the bag. He wondered how he could stop the Wasa from ever hurting his family again.

Bobi's parents called for him to return to their hut in the tree. They called and called up through each main tree trunk that led higher into the branches. He could not be found. They both became apprehensive and scared. Bobi's father had a bad feeling about where Bobi might have gone. The family had uncanny ways of knowing where each other were located, and Bobi's father could feel him outside of the tree.

Bobi had found a small dead branch and was approaching the Wasa nest. The sound coming from the nest started to intensify the closer he came. Then, with a sudden burst of noise, the Wasa streamed out of the hole at the bottom of the nest. They started to swarm directly at Bobi. He raised the branch, determined to destroy as many as he could. His father came running into the clearing, shouting for Bobi to run.

The swarm enveloped Bobi, and he closed his eyes tightly, thinking to himself that the Wasa should all go away, back to their nest, and was about to start swinging the branch, but he didn't. Finally, the noise of the Wasa began to diminish, and they all began returning to the nest. Bobi opened his eyes in time to see the last Wasa crawl into the hole. Bobi's father, standing not too far away, was amazed. He stood in awe while watching the spectacle.

Bobi and his father walked together back to their home. They did not speak, but each tried to fathom what had happened that day. Finally, they returned and climbed up the tree. His father explained what he had seen to Bobi's mother. After this, Bobi explained what had happened in Yabuut's room with the shrinking bumps. His parents told him to retire to his room to get some rest, for it had been a long day. Bobi thought this was a good idea.

Bobi's parents sat on chairs carved into the branch of their Oaka, each staring up into the evening sky.

"It doesn't happen very often, and I can't remember it happening in the last 1000 cycles," his father said.

"I agree, but what you have seen and what he has told us could mean only one thing," she replied.
"A Chosen One he is," they said together.

***

The translation is left wanting, and more than this could not be obtained from the recovered books. Even though they were in metal boxes, they had deteriorated terribly from their time in space. Another mining ship is due to be sent to this area and will have instructions to look for possibly more artifacts of the Avdanoorkian race.

A Child's Dragon

Children, Children, can you see
Three fuzzy dragons in that tree
Two are brown, and one is blue
I think they've come to play with you.

They jump around from limb to limb
And to the pond to take a swim
Don't worry, for they will not bite
They only peck for bug's delight.

Their feathers shine just like scales
With longer feathers on their tales
They have wings and small-clawed feet
They do not roar but sometimes tweet.

Now dragons in a tree seem strange
So, I think, my mind I'll change
There are no dragons in that tree
There are only birds that I can see.

But many years before your birth
They were dragons of the earth

Large and small with skin and scale
And like a snake was their long tail.

So do not fear, but understand
That they no longer walk the land
Small they are, just things to see
Birds, just singing in a tree.

Just think of how, way in the past
Their song a deep and throaty blast
How could their roar become so weak?
Ten million years did make them meek.

Now sit so still, hold out your hand
And with luck they'll come and land
In your palm they'll sing for you
Songs from birds both brown and blue.

Let it Snow

The snowflakes fell upon my hand
And others fell out on the land
And piled up, one on one
Until the winter storm was done.

Tree limbs sagged from all the weight
It snowed so much; it snowed so late
The street was covered twelve inches deep
You couldn't walk; you had to leap.

It beautiful to see the snow
See it fall and watch it grow
Into deep layers everywhere
On the houses and in the square.

Each flake a crystal from the sky
No two alike could be a lie
But if the two are just the same
The complaint would still be lame.

Now reality has just set in
There is no other way to spin

The truth I see lies just ahead
I cannot just return to bed.

I must get out and shovel the snow
There are places I must go
The plow went by to clear the street
Guess what happened nice and neat.
Where the driveway meets the street
It's two feet deep now; what a treat
There's no way I can get out
There's no use to sit and pout.

When I'm done, I'll look outside
And see the work I've done with pride
Sip hot cocoa on the couch
If it snows again, I'll be a grouch.

Starry Nights

My granddad told me that late at night
he could see the stars so bright
Now cars and trucks and bright lights all
in the parking lot, in the shopping mall.

lights line the streets up and down
there's neon bulbs all over town
stars are few up in the sky
there's ten or twelve you can't deny.

so when we want to gaze at night
we go up north; it's quite a sight
no city lights to dim the stars
now there's a billion, even Mars.

I see the stars; they are everywhere
they wink and blink, and as I stare
I can see the Milky Way
across the sky above the bay.

it's great to see the stars at night

away from town and all its blight
when I grow up, I think I'll find
a place that's dark and call it mine.

then I can show my kids the stars
and if they're good, I'll show them Mars.

Water

Beneath the surface, very deep
There may be water, and it will seep.

From the rocks below the ground
Make sure the well is deep and round.

There's enough for everyone
Share with all those in the sun.

No one shall thirst; it is the rule
This well becomes our village tool.

Around this well, our dwellings build
Our children's safety is now fulfilled.

Now, if a stranger comes along
And needs some water for their voyage long.

We'll give it freely because we know
It's only right for us to show.

The proper kindness to all others

For sure, in life, we are all brothers.

And for the kindness we do show
A place in heaven we will go.

Poop

I have a feeling deep down inside
From my bum, a ship will ride
I'm just too busy to stop and go
I know I should, I know, I know.

It's coming soon; it's very near
But it's part of me; it's very dear.

Mom said to go, get in the room
That porcelain chair, it looks like doom
But in my pants, there is lots of room!

I'll keep it close, just down below
Cept for the stink, no one would know.

But yet someday not far away
I'll flush the poop that went astray.

Hey Mom, look at this. Is that, OK?
What do you mean? "Hurray, Hurray!"

You'd think I just put out a fire

Me growing up, that's her desire.

42

Invitation

Come one come all, to this fine place.
It's moderate, not so fast paced.
You'll really like the stuff we do.
We try to write things, just for you.

Or possibly, you could try.
We don't care if you're small fry.
Most of us, have just begun,
To write things down, just for fun.

Some are young, and some are old.
We don't care. To write is bold!
Some use names that are unreal.
Other names are the real deal.

Some tell stories, others rhyme.
Write what you want, you've got the time.
Write for school, or to impress,
That girl you think is a bright princess.

It doesn't matter where you live.
It only matters, that you give,

Some time and effort, to your story.
It doesn't matter if it's gory.

But you need to spell, and follow rules,
And for writing there, are many tools,
That let the reader, see your story,
In all its beauty, or all its glory.

So, you've told me, that your way too shy,
But I insist that you just try.
You'll find it fun, and good escape,
To write of heroes, or an ape.
Someone had to write, you see,
For Superman, and Kong to be.

You never know, what's deep inside,
Please, I still insist you try.
And we will read what you have written.
From the pen, you might get bitten.

And down the road, when you've been printed.
Remember reading this, that hinted,
All you need, is to get started,
With effort, that must be wholehearted.

No Need for Speed

Papa! She said, Yes, my dear?
Papa, your instructions are not so clear.

Listen to me, look at my face
I'll tell you again, not to race.

But Papa I need, to get there fast.
I just don't want to be the last.

I don't care if we're the last.
My racing days have long since passed.

Now, I like it, nice and slow
At your speed, I shall not go.

I'm sorry, you can't stand the pace.
I'll slow down, and we won't race.

Thanks for your kind, understanding.
I'm sorry that, I'm so demanding.

But this wheelchair, you see.

Can't take the speed, you're pushing me.

The Hole

I've found a little
Hole in me,
It's right out there
For all to see.

Everybody has one
It's plain as plain can be,
It's right there in the middle,
Where everyone can see.

It's always there,
When I look down.
It's really small,
And really round.

They say they'll get it,
To make me squeal.
But I think they're,
Not so real.

Cause it never,
Goes away.

I think it's really,
Here to stay.

I just don't know,
What it does,
But lots of time it's
Full of fuzz.

I really do not like that hole,
It's not like things I've hated.
Now I think it can be said,
Bellybuttons are overrated.

When Exactly?

Circular in shape,
Just like a tire.
Two words inscribed,
Not to inspire.

I will do it, when I can,
I just don't have time right now,
I'll do it when I can,
I don't know when or how.

Where is that little coin?
I'll hand it right to you.
So, when you ask me one more time,
You'll know that it is true.

That if I find it lying there,
I'll pick it up right quick,
And when you read it in your hand
You will get a kick.

Cause then you'll know, the work you want,
And just when, I will do it.

I'll get it done, although a ton.
When I get, a *round* "**TO IT**"

WORDS

I used some words
I heard at school.
My mom fell off
Her kitchen stool.

They said them in
A real low voice.
We all laughed
I had no choice.

If I said those
Words were bad.
They might not like me
I'd be sad.

And now those words
Seem really mean.
Hateful words
From some bad dream.

When said to some

It makes them cry.
I thought it fun
I don't know why.

But then I thought
If said to me.
I 'd feel bad
So now I see.

How some words
Really strong.
Used without thought
Can be so wrong.

They make you feel
So very sad.
I guess those words
Are really bad.

I just decided
It's up to me
To use only words
That I can see

Will make you smile
And be happy
Even if they sound
Real sappy.

I'd rather see you,
Smile at me.
A friend forever,
Meant to be.

Don't miss out!

Visit the website below and you can sign up to receive emails whenever J.J. Smiley publishes a new book. There's no charge and no obligation.

https://books2read.com/r/B-A-NBSE-PFNY

Also by J.J. Smiley

All That Remains
A Knack for Trouble
The Itch
Run!
Coven; Short Stories of Sci-fi and Fantasy
The Tree
Beware Pleiades

About the Author

Disappointed with titles that I read or watched in the theatre, it was time to write my own adventures. Just writing for personal pleasure at first and then publishing, has now become a joyful pastime.

My wife who is always watching my back convinced me to go to press.

www.ingramcontent.com/pod-product-compliance
Lightning Source LLC
Chambersburg PA
CBHW032023140726
47988CB00017BA/1380